D1448631

MARYLEBONE TO RICKMANSWORTH

Vic Mitchell and Keith Smith

MP Middleton Press

Cover picture: A down Metropolitan Line train passes through Neasden station in 1956, as a BR 2-6-0 approaches the junction of the main lines. The cross on the tender shows that it will take the Wembley Stadium loop, thus its next trip from Marylebone will be smokebox first. The double track on the right was used by South of England trains. (N.W.Sprinks)

Published February 2005

ISBN 1 904474 49 7

© Middleton Press, 2005

Design David Pede

Published by
>*Middleton Press*
>*Easebourne Lane*
>*Midhurst, West Sussex*
>*GU29 9AZ*

Tel: 01730 813169
Fax: 01730 812601
Email: info@middletonpress.co.uk
www.middletonpress.co.uk

Printed & bound by Biddles Ltd, Kings Lynn

INDEX

ACKNOWLEDGEMENTS

We are very grateful for the assistance received from many of those mentioned in the credits also to P.G.Barnes, A.E.Bennett, J.E.Connor, L.Crosier, G.Croughton, R.J.Harley, D.Hyde, B.S.Jennings, N.Langridge, Dr J.S.Manners, J.H.Meredith, Mr D. and Dr S.Salter, M.J.Stretton, D.Wilson and particularly our ever supportive wives, Barbara Mitchell and Janet Smith.

I. The GWR's route map of 1910 omits to mention the Metropolitan Railway's joint operation with the GCR.

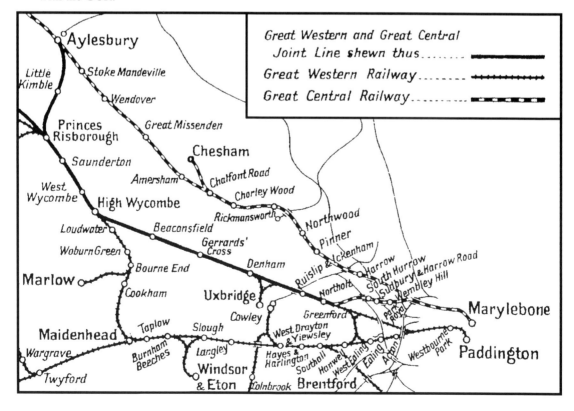

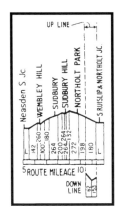

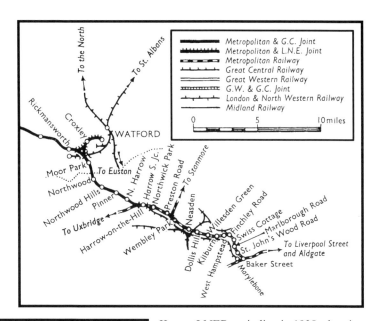

II.   LNER main line in 1938, showing previous ownerships. (Railway Magazine)

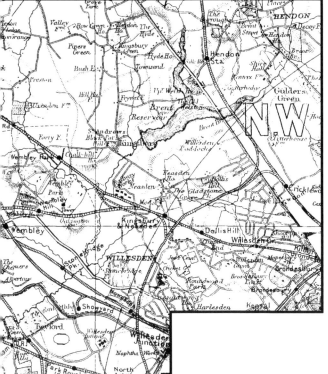

III.   Bacon's map of about 1910 shows the then rural area of the route at 1 inch to 1 mile.

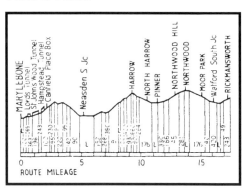

GEOGRAPHICAL SETTING

Much of the first two miles of the route tunnels under the high ground forming the southern part of Hampstead Heath. After three miles of climbing, the line descends to Neasden to cross the Brent Valley and then climbs to reach the elevated residential area of Harrow.

An undulating course continues across London Clay, and the Colne Valley is traversed about a mile before reaching the old country town of Rickmansworth, which is situated on Chalk at the base of the dip slope of the Chiltern Hills.

The Watford branch is on the north side of the valley of the River Colne and is close to the Grand Union Canal before crossing it, half a mile west of the terminus.

The Northolt route passes over the River Brent near Wembley Stadium and reaches a summit at Sudbury Hill before descending to join the route from Paddington.

Most of the London end of the route was in Middlesex for the majority of its life, the section north of Northwood being in Hertfordshire.

The maps are to the scale of 25ins to 1 mile, with north at the top, unless otherwise indicated.

HISTORICAL BACKGROUND

Eventually to form part of the Circle Line, the Metropolitan Railway's route between Farringdon Street and Paddington opened in 1863. The Metropolitan & St. Johns Wood Railway branched north from it at Baker Street and came into use on 13th April 1868.

The line was extended from St. Johns Wood thus: to West Hampstead on 30th June 1879, to Willesden Green on 24th November 1879, to Harrow-on-the-Hill on 2nd August 1880, to Pinner on 25th May 1885, to Rickmansworth on 1st September 1887 and on to Chesham in 1889, Aylesbury eventually being reached in 1892. The Met had absorbed the M&SWR in 1882, having operated services for it from the outset.

Meanwhile the Manchester, Sheffield & Lincolnshire Railway had expansionist plans aimed on London and its name was changed to the Great Central Railway in 1897. It made an agreement with the Met to operate over its route south of Quainton Road (which is north of Aylesbury) to a new terminus at Marylebone, this coming into use on 15th March 1899. North of Harrow, the line was jointly operated by the Metropolitan & Great Central Committee after its formation in 1906. Each railway undertook most maintenance for alternate periods of five years. South of Harrow South Junction, the tracks continued to be owned by the Met, but the GCR obtained a long lease on the western pair.

The plan proved unsatisfactory for the GCR and it made alternative arrangements in Buckinghamshire, by using part of the Great Western Railway's 1906 direct route between London and Birmingham. The GCR built a line from Neasden westwards to Northolt to reach the GCR/GWR joint line, which opened on 2nd April 1906.

The Met started an electrification programme in 1904 on its underground lines, extending to Harrow and its new line from there to Uxbridge. The Met's next route expansion was to Watford, this taking place on 5th January 1925. This was electrified from the outset and at the same time conductor rails were laid to Rickmansworth. They were extended to Amersham on 9th September 1961.

The Met came under the London Passenger Transport Board (LT) in 1933, the GCR having become a constituent of the London & North Eastern Railway (LNER) in 1923. The lines north of Rickmansworth were operated by the LNER from 1st November 1937.

Upon nationalisation in 1948, the LNER became largely the Eastern Region of British Railways, but the former LNER-operated services within this volume were transferred to the London Midland Region on 1st February 1958 and then to the Western Region on 11th October 1987. They became part of the Thames & Chiltern area of Network SouthEast at that time. With the advent of privatisation, a franchise was let on 21st July 1996 to M40 Trains for Chiltern Railways to operate all services from Marylebone for seven years. Owing to its success, an extension to 2021 followed.

Stanmore branch

The Met opened this line from Wembley Park on 10th December 1932, using full size electric stock. Tube trains have operated it since 20th November 1939, when such tunnels were completed between Baker Street and Finchley Road. This service was part of the Bakerloo Line of LT, the southern terminus of which had been Elephant & Castle since 1906.

The branch became the northern part of the Jubilee Line on 1st May 1979, the other extremity of which was eventually to be at Stratford. New tunnels were provided south from Baker Street to Charing Cross from that date.

PASSENGER SERVICES

The April 1880 timetable showed trains at 10 minute intervals to Kilburn & Brondesbury and every 30 minutes to Willesden Green, with fewer on Sundays. The same frequency applied upon extension to Harrow-on-the-Hill in 1880, Pinner in 1885 and Rickmansworth in 1887.

Following the extension of services to Aylesbury in 1892, the 30 minute interval was cut back to Harrow, with trains approximately hourly north thereof except at peak times. They were still irregular by 1898, particularly on Sundays.

There were few changes to Met services with the advent of GCR trains in 1899. The latter departed from Marylebone at 5.15, 8.0, 10.0am, 12.0 noon, 12.8, 1.30, 4.0, 6.15, 7.5, 7.45 and 10.30pm. There were four on Sundays. Most ran non-stop over the route, but a few called at Harrow-on-the-Hill, "when required to take up".

The opening of the Northolt line in 1906 brought 14 departures from Marylebone, 6 of which were stopping trains. The Sunday figures were 6 and 5. The number of GCR trains running via Harrow-on-the-Hill was reduced from 11 to 6, with only one on Sundays. There was also a railmotor service from Marylebone to South Harrow of nine trains, weekdays only.

By 1922, Rickmansworth was receiving 21 trains from Baker Street and 24 from Marylebone, on weekdays. On Sundays, the figures were 14 and 6. South Harrow had only four railmotor trips (all terminating there), but the number of through local trains had increased to 18, with 7 on Sundays.

Electrification of the Rickmansworth route brought little alteration to the irregularity of the service and Watford was provided with an equally erratic timetable, with arrivals on Mondays to Fridays at 7.36, 7.49, 8.17, 8.40, 9.19, 9.29, 9.52, 10.33, 11.12, 11.50, 12.30, 1.10, 1.51, 2.30, 3.10, 3.37, 4.30, 5.6, 5.15, 5.30, 5.47, 6.25, 6.46, 7.0, 7.5, 7.20, 8.10, 8.50, 9.30, 10.10, 10.49, 11.30 and 12.52.

The 1947 timetable for the Northolt route on weekdays showed 23 stopping trains and 10 fast. There were 11 trains from Marylebone to Rickmansworth in that period, most continuing to Aylesbury or beyond. There were also three fast to that town. The electric services were listed as "at frequent intervals throughout the day".

Long distance daytime trains over the route ceased on 2nd January 1960 and no trains ran north of Aylesbury after 4th September 1966. The timetable was recast with the elimination of steam traction between Rickmansworth and Amersham on 9th September 1961. LT services between these places had been partially electric from 12th September 1960. In addition to "a frequent service" by LT, there was a basic hourly frequency of DMUs from Marylebone. The latter also applied to an all-stations service via Northolt, but these trains ran non-stop to West Ruislip off-peak from 1964. The Wembley Stadium (Complex) stop was restored later.

The Marylebone-Aylesbury service via Rickmansworth was increased to two per hour from 1990 and the Marylebone-High Wycombe route received the same enhancement in 1991, only to be increased to three in 1995. Passenger figures on Chiltern Railways rose from 5m in 1994 to 12m in 2004, the number of coaches in the fleet doubling in that period.

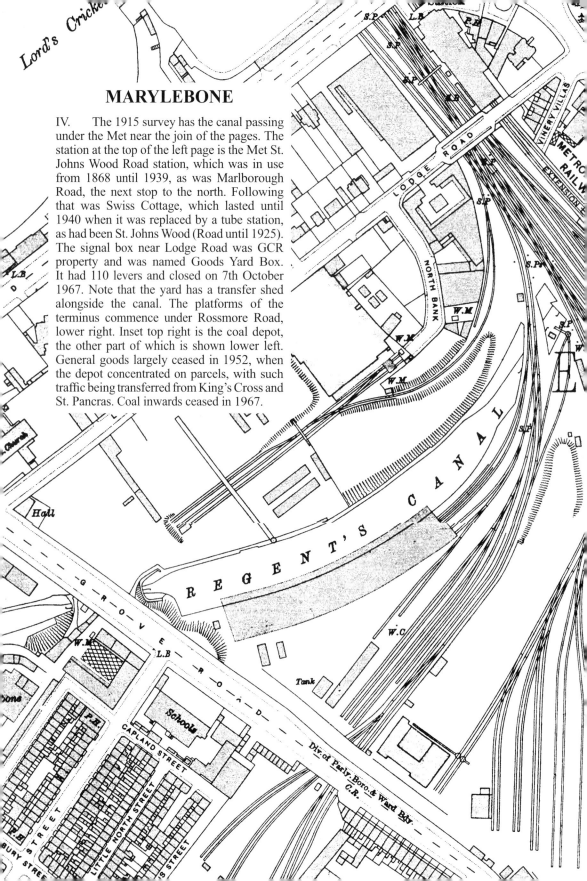

MARYLEBONE

IV.   The 1915 survey has the canal passing under the Met near the join of the pages. The station at the top of the left page is the Met St. Johns Wood Road station, which was in use from 1868 until 1939, as was Marlborough Road, the next stop to the north. Following that was Swiss Cottage, which lasted until 1940 when it was replaced by a tube station, as had been St. Johns Wood (Road until 1925). The signal box near Lodge Road was GCR property and was named Goods Yard Box. It had 110 levers and closed on 7th October 1967. Note that the yard has a transfer shed alongside the canal. The platforms of the terminus commence under Rossmore Road, lower right. Inset top right is the coal depot, the other part of which is shown lower left. General goods largely ceased in 1952, when the depot concentrated on parcels, with such traffic being transferred from King's Cross and St. Pancras. Coal inwards ceased in 1967.

1.   This postcard was produced soon after the opening in 1899 and it includes all four platforms and the off-centre cab road. Gracious, spacious and generally peaceful was an apt description until recent times. Platform 1 is on the right and there is a crossover behind the bookstall.
(Lens of Sutton coll.)

2.   A westward view across the cab road reveals that the concourse was designed to serve more platforms than the four built. The entrance to nos 3 and 4 is on the right and the Bakerloo Line booking office was added nearby. Its station opened in 1907 as "Great Central", a name used until 1917. (Lens of Sutton coll.)

3.	Inside the booking hall was joinery of the highest quality and much of this can still be enjoyed, albeit incorporated inside a shop. Passenger revenue was a disappointment to GCR directors, but freight returns were impressive. (British Railways)

4.	This southward view has Rossmore Road bridge in the background and the 100-lever Station Box being restored after a V1 attack on 17th July 1944. Part of the goods shed (right) had been demolished by Nazi bombers in April 1941. The platform on the left was for fish and milk traffic. (British Railways)

5.   The restored box was photographed on 5th December 1944, but in the background are the ruins of the carriage washer, the oil gasworks and some dwellings. Some 507 houses occupied by 3073 people had earlier been destroyed by the GCR. The area had included some fashionable squares. (British Railways)

6.   Smoke from a departing loco obscures part of Rossmore Road bridge as class N2 0-6-2T no. 9516 arrives at platform 2 in about 1947. The delivery vans are standing on the cab road. (A.W.V.Mace/Milepost 92½)

7.	A 54ft 7ins turntable and this coaling plant was situated on the east side of the main line (see map) north of Station Box, which is in the background of this picture from 6th August 1948. It includes nos. 9823, 9800 and E1298. (V.R.Webster/E.Hancock)

8.	A 70ft turntable was built in about 1937 east of the goods shed and was eventually moved to Fort William in June 2000. On the left are the platforms and also the vacuum hose, which took power from the engine's braking system to the cylinder on the right - and thence the turning mechanism. Class B1 no. 1187 was only one year old when photographed in July 1948. (G.Powell/GERS)

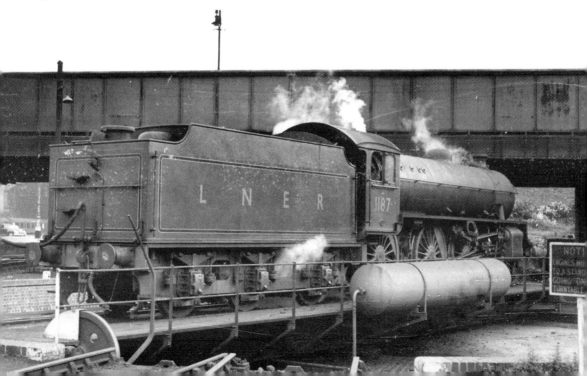

9.   A portal crane of 35-ton capacity was erected at the southern point of the goods yard and for 13-14th May 1961 was used to carry the banners relating to the golden jubilee of the Institution of Locomotive Engineers. Among the many exhibits were class 9F 2-10-0 no. 92220 *Evening Star* (left) and ex-Midland Railway 4-4-0 no. 1000. (S.P.Derek)

10.   Three photos from the 1970s allow us to travel the full length of the cab road in a period of terminal decline, in more than one sense. Closure notices were exhibited in 1984, the plan being to divert the few remaining local services to Baker Street or Paddington and to convert the area to a coach station. (M.A.King/E.Hancock)

11.   On the left is the arch for departing cabs and on the right is a DMU at platform 4. The closure scheme involved converting the tracks to roads, easily done as the structures had been built to the large European loading gauge. The GCR had initially planned running to Paris. Automatic ticket barriers came into use in December 1997. (M.A.King/E.Hancock)

12.   Cabs once emerged from the arch, while others stood under the porte-cochère. To the left is the covered way to the lavish Great Central Hotel. This became a convalescent home in World War I and government offices in the next conflict. It became the home of the Railway Executive in 1948 and subsequently the British Railways Board until 1986. It is now a hotel again and is a listed structure, as is the station. (D.Thompson)

13.   With sun visor down, a four-car Derby-built DMU leaves platform 1 on a shunting move on 15th May 1978. The curved cab road is behind the rear coach; it is also shown on the map. The other units are berthed in sidings. This and the next view are from the signal box. (F.Hornby)

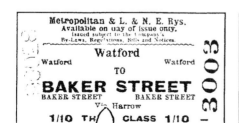

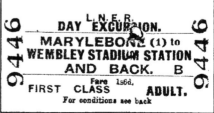

14.	The camera was turned slightly to the left to include both sheds of the diesel depot and part of the dock again. These DMUs were introduced on the route on 23rd January 1961. (F.Hornby)

15.	This northward view from December 1983 features the replacement signal box, which remained in use until superseded by a panel in September 1990. (J.G.S.Smith/E.Hancock)

16.   The closure threat was lifted in 1986 and the formation of Network SouthEast that year brought the start of a remarkable revival period. The cab road was replaced with two tracks in 1989 and the western roof span was removed in 1990 but its canopy was saved to go over the new platform 4. Compare this January 1992 panorama with picture no. 10. The featureless tower (Melbury House) was used as railway offices and was demolished in 1995. (M.Turvey)

17.   Steam specials were operated quite often from 1985, notably to Stratford-upon-Avon. However, ex-LNER class V2 2-6-2 no. 60800 *Green Arrow* was present on 14th March 1999 as part of the station's centenary celebrations. Steam activity soon ended. However, long distance traffic increased steadily, the Birmingham frequency becoming two per hour in December 2004 and a regular service to Stratford-upon-Avon started at that time, basically one train every two hours. Plans were made for two additional platforms on the site of the sidings. (S.P.Derek)

NORTH OF MARYLEBONE

18.   Ex-LMS 4-6-2 no. 46229 *Duchess of Hamilton* has emerged from the 1606yd long St. Johns Wood Tunnel with "The Shakespeare Limited" on 26th May 1985. The other end of the tunnel is shown at the top of the Marylebone map; its construction involved lifting part of Lords Cricket Ground in 1896 and replacing it for the 1897 season. The train is passing over the lines featured in the *Euston to Harrow* album immediately east of South Hampstead station. It will soon enter Hampstead Tunnel. (D.T.Rowe)

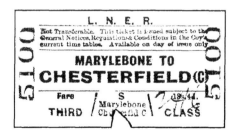

L. N. E. R.

Not Transferable. This ticket is issued subject to the General Notices, Regulations & Conditions in the Coy's current time tables. Available on day of issue only

MARYLEBONE TO
CHESTERFIELD (C)

Fare	S	
THIRD	Marylebone Chesterfield C	CLASS

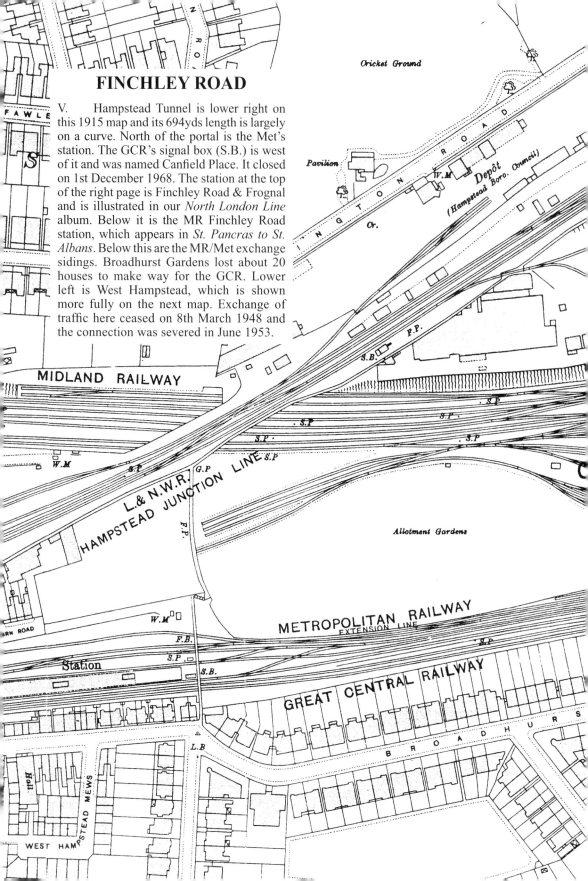

FINCHLEY ROAD

V.　　Hampstead Tunnel is lower right on this 1915 map and its 694yds length is largely on a curve. North of the portal is the Met's station. The GCR's signal box (S.B.) is west of it and was named Canfield Place. It closed on 1st December 1968. The station at the top of the right page is Finchley Road & Frognal and is illustrated in our *North London Line* album. Below it is the MR Finchley Road station, which appears in *St. Pancras to St. Albans*. Below this are the MR/Met exchange sidings. Broadhurst Gardens lost about 20 houses to make way for the GCR. Lower left is West Hampstead, which is shown more fully on the next map. Exchange of traffic here ceased on 8th March 1948 and the connection was severed in June 1953.

Cricket Ground

Pavilion

W.M.

Depôt
(Hampstead Boro. Council)

F.P.

S.B.

MIDLAND RAILWAY

W.M.

S.P.

S.P.

S.P.

S.P.

S.P.

S.P.

L. & N.W.R. HAMPSTEAD JUNCTION LINE

G.P

S.P

F.P.

Allotment Gardens

W.M.

F.B.

Station

S.P.

S.B.

METROPOLITAN RAILWAY
EXTENSION LINE

S.P

GREAT CENTRAL RAILWAY

B R O A D H U R S

L.B

Hall

WEST HAMPSTEAD MEWS

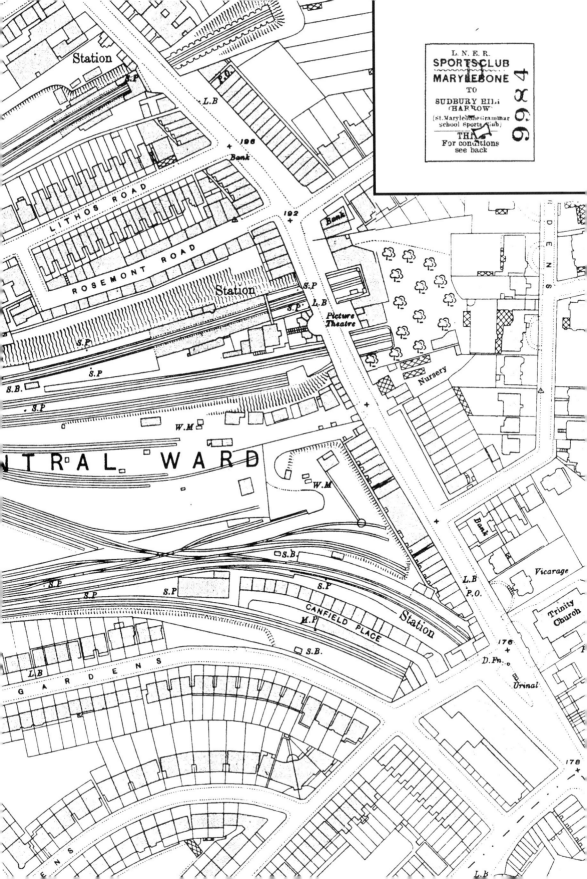

Station

S.P

P.O.

L.B

LITHOS ROAD

196

Bank

ROSEMONT ROAD

192

Bank

Station

S.P

L.B

Picture
Theatre

Nursery

S.P

S.P

S.B.

S.P

W.M.

N T R A L   W A R D

W.M

Bank

Vicarage

L.B
P.O.

S.B.

S.P

S.P

S.P

S.P

Station

Trinity
Church

CANFIELD PLACE

M.P.

176

D.Fn.

S.B.

Urinal

G A R D E N S

L.B

178

E N S

L.B

19.   The Met station was enlarged in 1938 so that the Bakerloo line tunnels could come to the surface here and use the centre two of the four new platforms. Wagons stand in the ex-MR goods yard as a down train departs for Watford in April 1962. The Met goods yard was open to public traffic from 1st January 1894 to 1st August 1941. The sidings were lifted in 1955. (J.C.Gillham)

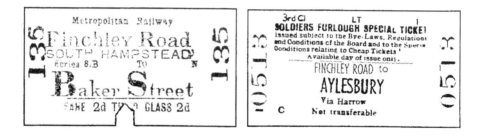

Metropolitan Railway
135 Finchley Road 135
SOUTH HAMPSTEAD
Series 8.B   To   N
Baker Street
FARE 2d THIRD CLASS 2d

3rd Cl   LT
SOLDIERS FURLOUGH SPECIAL TICKET
Issued subject to the Bye-Laws, Regulations
and Conditions of the Board and to the Special
Conditions relating to Cheap Tickets
Available day of issue only.
FINCHLEY ROAD to
AYLESBURY
Via Harrow
C   Not transferable

WEST HAMPSTEAD

20.   The original up platform became an island on 13th June 1897 to allow construction of the GCR tracks. Further rebuilding in 1938 made provision for Bakerloo trains, but Metropolitan services continued to call until December 1940. The former GCR tracks are on the left of this 1962 panorama and in the background are the points to the reversal siding. (J.C.Gillham)

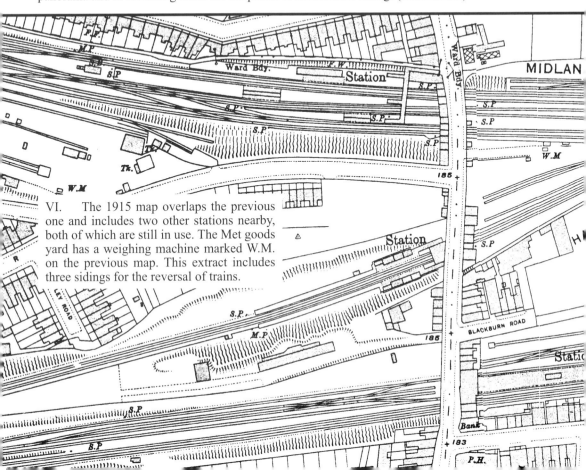

VI.   The 1915 map overlaps the previous one and includes two other stations nearby, both of which are still in use. The Met goods yard has a weighing machine marked W.M. on the previous map. This extract includes three sidings for the reversal of trains.

KILBURN

21.   This westward view from 26th November 1977 has a crane in the gap created by the removal of the original 1879 bridge over Kilburn High Road. The arched bridge is from 1899; the nearest one still carries in large iron letters METROPOLITAN RAILWAY 1914. The Met quadrupling from Finchley Road to the bridge over the LNWR (beyond the left border of map VI) was completed on 30th November 1913 and was extended to Willesden Green on 31st May 1915. However, the section from there to Neasden came into use earlier, on 4th January 1914. In the distance is the bridge for the North London Line. There is another entrance to the station in Christchurch Road (right) and the centre bridge over this was replaced at the same time. (J.C.Gillham)

22.   A new island platform for Bakerloo services came into use on 20th November 1939 and is seen on 2nd October 2004 as a train proceeds towards Marylebone behind gigantic weeds, guaranteed to shed leaves on the lines. (V.Mitchell)

WILLESDEN GREEN

VII.   The goods yard remained in use until 3rd January 1966, it being operated by the LMR from 1962. A bay was completed on the north side in 1906. This 1935 map includes the tram route which is featured in *Edgware and Willesden Tramways* (Middleton Press).

23.   Two extra platforms were available by 1914 for the advent of the Met quadrupling and from 1939 the centre ones were used for tube trains. Metropolitan Line services seldom used the outer ones after 1940. This is a 1979 view towards London, the Marylebone lines being behind the wall on the right. (J.C.Gillham)

24.   This imposing entrance was completed in 1925, its cream glazed terracotta tiling being adorned with gilded lettering. It is the finest exterior on the route and was photographed in 1994. Thankfully the intrusive trees have been removed. (F.Hornby)

DOLLIS HILL

25.   The station was opened on 1st October 1909 in response to housing development and the platform was repositioned in 1938 in readiness for Bakerloo services. One such train waits to depart north in April 1979, the month before the Jubilee Line came into being. (J.C.Gillham)

26.   Approaching Dollis Hill on 6th October 1954 is no. L46 with a coal train from Neasden. This was one of a batch of four 0-4-4Ts purchased by the Met from Hawthorn Leslie in 1900-01. An earlier E class survivor is no. 1. The Met had about 35 steam locomotives in 1925. LT locos worked goods trains between Neasden Yard and Willesden Green until 1962. (T.Wright)

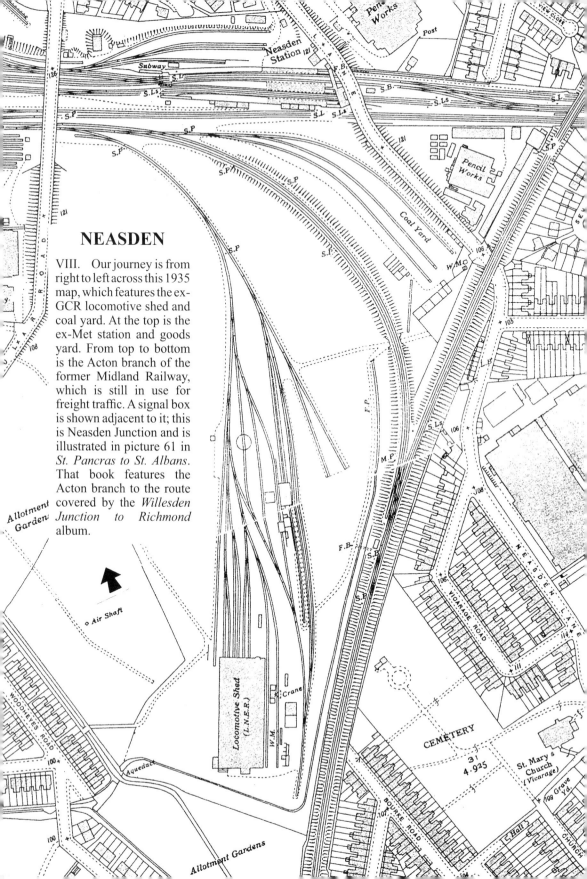

NEASDEN

VIII.   Our journey is from right to left across this 1935 map, which features the ex-GCR locomotive shed and coal yard. At the top is the ex-Met station and goods yard. From top to bottom is the Acton branch of the former Midland Railway, which is still in use for freight traffic. A signal box is shown adjacent to it; this is Neasden Junction and is illustrated in picture 61 in *St. Pancras to St. Albans*. That book features the Acton branch to the route covered by the *Willesden Junction to Richmond* album.

Neasden Station

27.   Opened as "Kingsbury & Neasden" in 1880, the names were reversed in 1910 and the suffix was dropped in 1932. This view of a down train behind a Beyer Peacock 4-4-0T is from the 1880s and shows only one siding. (Railway Magazine)

28.   Heading the 3.15pm Marylebone to Sheffield on 27th June 1914 is no. 259. It had been built at Gorton in 1906 as GCR class 8D no. 259 *King Edward VII* and was scrapped in 1947. The earthworks have begun for the bridge which would eventually carry the North Circular Road. On the left are new platforms for the extra Met lines. (R.M.Casserley coll.)

29.   A train of F stock passes through on its way from Uxbridge to Baker Street on 9th August 1961, with the bowstring girders of the North Circular bridge in the background. On the left, a driver has emerged from the staff subway (see map) provided in 1922 and still in use. (T.J.Edgington)

30.   Crossing the road outside the station entrance, we look east to see the bridge carrying the Acton branch from Cricklewood, top right on the map. Electric locomotives of this type ran regularly between London and Rickmansworth in the period 1925 to 1961. However, this picture is from 26th May 1963 and shows one of the survivors of a class of 20, no. 5 *John Hampden* on a special train. It now resides in London's Transport Museum. (L.W.Rowe/D.T.Rowe)

31.   A panorama from the other side of the bridge in 1971 includes the 1880 down platform building seen on the right of picture no. 27. The lines from Marylebone are in the foreground and curving left beyond the arch are the tracks for High Wycombe trains. (M.A.King/E.Hancock)

Neasden Shed

33.   Some details are evident as 0-6-2T no. 5913 waits for its next duty on 6th June 1925. The N5 class was produced in 1891-1901. The code became 34E in 1949, as a sub-shed to Kings Cross and, in 1958, 14D as a sub-shed to Cricklewood. It closed on 17th June 1961 and was demolished in September 1967. (H.C.Casserley)

32.   The GCR constructed this massive six-road shed in anticipation of great traffic growth. It is seen in 1913 in its rural setting, over six miles from the terminus it served.
(R.M.Casserley coll.)

34.   Near the coaling plant on 23rd June 1948 was class O7 no. 63188, one of 200 2-8-0s produced for the War Department from 1943 onwards and taken into LNER stock in 1946. In 1954, the shed had four LMS class 4 2-6-4Ts, six LNER class A3 4-6-2s, seven LNER class B1 4-6-0s, three LNER class C13 4-4-2Ts, 36 LNER class L1 2-6-4Ts, ten LNER class N5 0-6-2Ts and ten BR class 4 2-6-0s. There were still 62 engines here in the early part of 1962.
(H.C.Casserley)

Neasden South Junction - southwards

35.   The station and its pitched roof building is in the background of all three photos. This one is from 1903 and shows 4-2-2 no. 968 coming off the single line from the engine shed and includes two GCR signal boxes on the right. See the cover picture for another view. (R.M.Casserley coll.)

36.   The former GCR coal yard is in the right background; it was in use from 25th July 1898 until 4th March 1968. In the left background is the ex-Met goods yard, which served from 1st January 1894 to April 1958. Passing through in the mid-1950s is T stock destined for Watford and ex-LNER 0-6-2T no. 69572 bound for the Wembley Stadium loop. This class N2 engine has condensing pipes and normally worked on the Kings Cross lines. Its destination board shows GORDON HILL, upside down. (N.W.Sprinks)

37.   On the right is double track to the engine shed. Ex-SR class H15 4-6-0 no. 30523 is creeping round the curve to the junction in 1956, with a Feltham to Neasden transfer freight. The engine shed site was in use as a stone terminal by Aggregate Industries in 2004. A single line sufficed for this and also for the curve to the Acton line. (N.W.Sprinks)

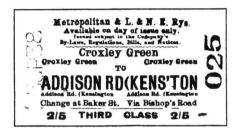

38. Now for three views from the other side of the North Circular Road, the first two being from 12th November 1967. This features Neasden South Junction box, which had 84 levers in use and closed in March 1990. The DMU is from High Wycombe and is about to join the line from Aylesbury. On the left are the extensive Neasden South sidings. (M.Dart)

39. No. D852 passes the box with a train diverted from Paddington. In the background are the chimneys of the power station built by the Met. The lines in the foreground allowed trains from Acton to run to High Wycombe, but they have had no direct access to the Rickmansworth line here. (M.Dart)

40.   The "Santa Steam Pullman" returns from High Wycombe on 13th December 1986 behind ex-LNER 4-6-2 no. 4472 *Flying Scotsman* and passes under the aptly named Great Central Way. The box had a 90-lever frame and was dismantled in October 1990 for reuse on the new GCR at Ruddington, near Nottingham. The spur to the left was to three little used sidings. (S.P.Derek)

Neasden Depot

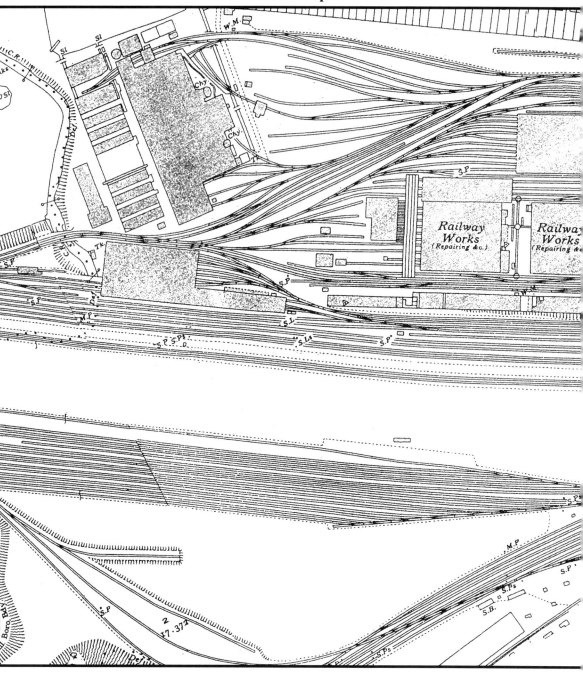

IX.   This map overlaps the left of the previous one and has Neasden South Junction box on the right and Neasden North Junction box on the left page, lower right. Two of the 15 parallel sidings above it remained in use in 2004 for Tibbett & Britten's Freight Terminal. The lines curving lower left are from Wembley Stadium. Upper left are the power station and engine shed built by the Met. Across the pages are its depot and works, where several of its steam locomotives were built.

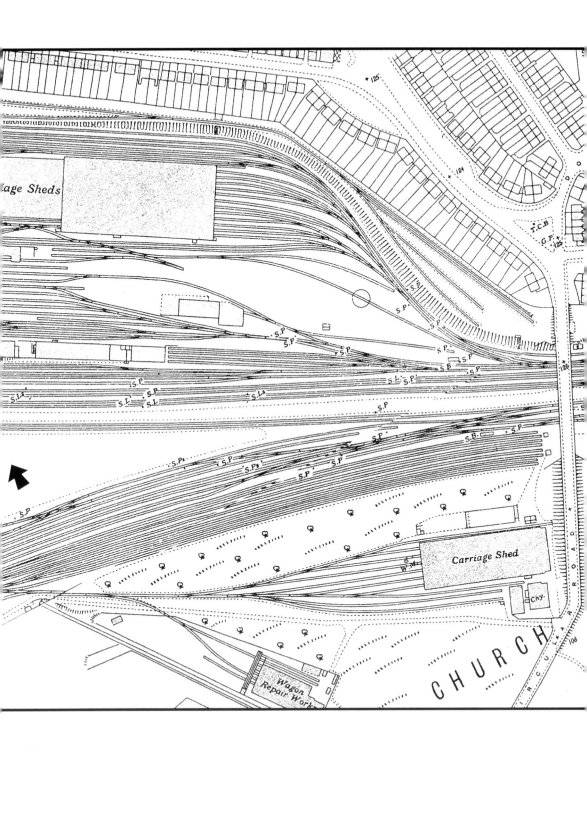

rage Sheds

Carriage Shed

CHURCH

Wagon Repair Works

41.   The east end of the depot is seen in about 1930, with one track apparently dedicated to steam traction and battery locomotives. (J.C.Gillham coll.)

42.   At the west end of the site was the coal stage and behind the camera was the original iron-clad engine shed. This was demolished in 1936 and a new one built to the north of it. Having its wheels cleaned on 1st July 1934 is 0-6-2T no. 93, being watered is 4-4-0T no. 49 and over the pit is 4-4-4T no. 104. (H.F.Wheeller/R.S.Carpenter)

43.   The replacement shed was recorded on 10th June 1957, along with the coal stack. The nearest track is Southbound Bakerloo. (D.B.Clayton)

44.   The mighty power station closed in 1968, after which time most current was drawn from the national grid. This westward view is from 1957 and includes first and second generation electric stock. LT's other power station at Lots Road, Chelsea, lasted until 21st October 2002. (T.Wright)

45.   From a similar viewpoint in December 1958, we witness no. 13 *Dick Whittington* shunting near the carriage washing plant. The footpath begins at the subway mentioned in caption 29. (T.Wright)

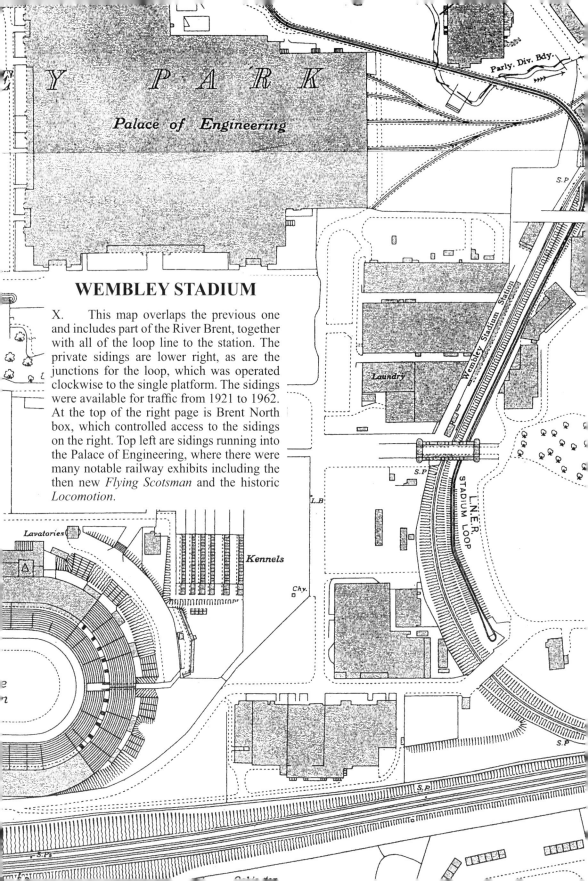

Y PARK

Palace of Engineering

Parly. Div. Bdy.

S.P

WEMBLEY STADIUM

X.   This map overlaps the previous one and includes part of the River Brent, together with all of the loop line to the station. The private sidings are lower right, as are the junctions for the loop, which was operated clockwise to the single platform. The sidings were available for traffic from 1921 to 1962. At the top of the right page is Brent North box, which controlled access to the sidings on the right. Top left are sidings running into the Palace of Engineering, where there were many notable railway exhibits including the then new *Flying Scotsman* and the historic *Locomotion*.

Laundry

Wembley Stadium Station

L.N.E.R. STADIUM LOOP

S.P

L.B

Lavatories

Kennels

Chy.

S.P

S.P

S.P

S.Ps

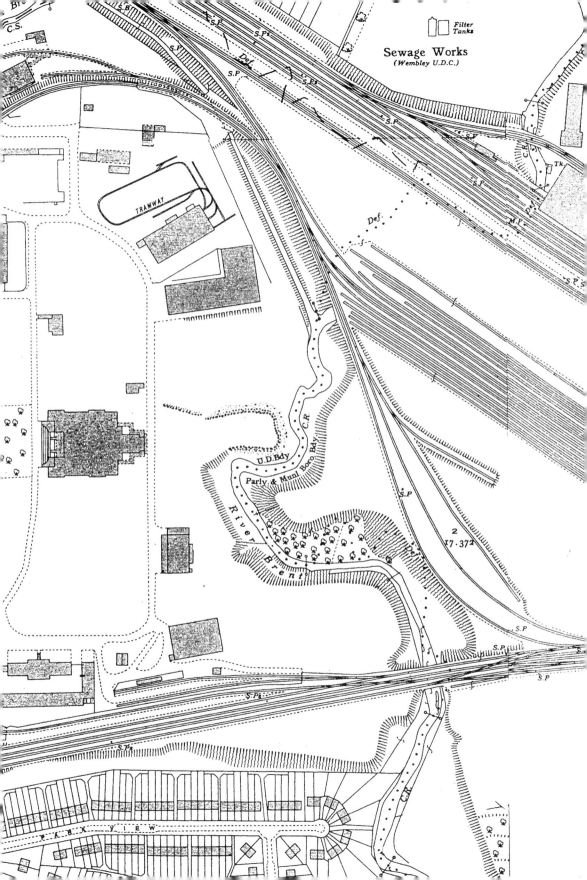

C.S.

Filter
Tanks

Sewage Works
(Wembley U.D.C.)

Tk.

TRAMWAY

Def

M.P.

C.R.

U.D.Bdy

Parly & Munl Boro Bdy

S.P

River Brent

2
17·37

Def

S.P

S.P.

S.P

S.P

S.P

S.P.

C.R.

PARK VIEW

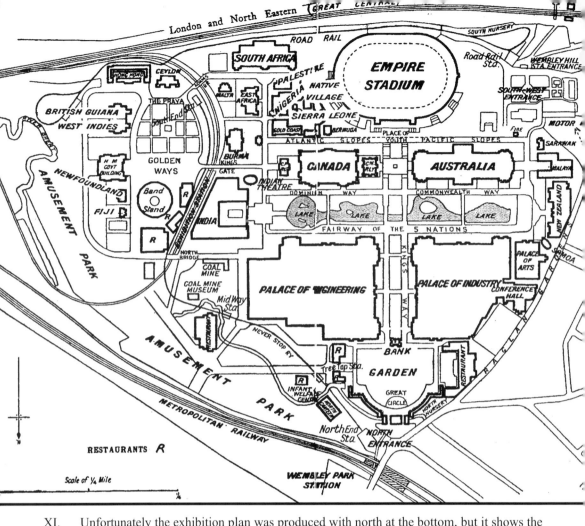

XI.   Unfortunately the exhibition plan was produced with north at the bottom, but it shows the Never Stop Railway in full. The trains had no crews and were propelled by screws between the rails. Their pitch varied to give the coaches a speed of 1mph at the platforms and over 20 between the stations. How crude today's travelators are in comparison.

47. The eight-coach platform was available for passenger use from 28th April 1923 to 18th May 1968, but only when events were taking place. Formal closure was on 1st September 1969 and demolition followed in 1974. (Lens of Sutton coll.)

48. A DMU squeals round the little used curve on 30th July 1966 on the occasion of the World Cup Final. Industrial premises spread over the trackbed after closure and little trace of it now remains. (T.Wright)

46. The loop had colour light signalling from the outset and trains could run every eight minutes, the journey from Marylebone taking 12 minutes. The British Empire Exhibition was held in 1924-25 and an LNER 0-6-2T approaches the Indian Pavilion on 4th July 1925. Two of the Never Stop coaches are included. They ran on concrete strips quoted as "2ft 10½ins gauge" and the bodies were later used on the Ashover Railway. (H.C.Casserley)

←

49.   Neasden North Junction box had 77 levers and is seen shortly after its closure on 15th October 1972. Its location is shown on map IX, left page lower. (M.A.King/E.Hancock)

50.   Brent North box (left) had about 20 levers and was in use until 21st May 1967. It is at the top of map X. No. 60090 *Grand Parade* is seen with "The South Yorkshireman" in the Spring of 1949, when it was temporarily allocated to Leicester. (D.Pearce coll.)

WEMBLEY HILL

Wembley Hill
Station

LONDON & NORTH EASTERN RAILWAY

OAKINGTON MANOR DRIVE

T.C.B.
Greyhound
(P.H.)

XII.   Part of the Empire Stadium is included on the previous map and a further section of it is on this 1937 extract. Note that two footbridges were provided to handle the crowds. The dock siding was not listed as a goods yard and so dates are not available.

51.   The main entrance was recorded on a postcard along with details of GCR non-stop expresses to Doncaster. The covered way allowed ticket inspection before entry to either platform. The station was "Wembley Hill" until 8th May 1978, "Wembley Complex" until 11th May 1987 and "Wembley Stadium" thereafter. We use the original name to avoid duplication of the present one. (Lens of Sutton coll.)

52.   The rural location is emphasised in this Edwardian postcard view, which includes the massive retaining wall in the cutting beyond the station. The long dock is close to the undeveloped Wembley Park. (Lens of Sutton coll.)

53.   The 6.15pm "Master Cutler" to Sheffield was hauled by class A3 4-6-2 no. 60108 *Gay Crusader* on 13th May 1953. Named trains were operated from 1947 to 1960 and included "Starlight Special" to Scotland and "The Orient" to Immingham Docks. The 31-lever signal box was open until 21st December 1969. (N.W.Sprinks)

54.   This 1962 view reveals the extensive provision for gentlemen at the east end of the building, the generous ventilator being the clue. Part of the western footbridge is also included. (J.C.Gillham)

55.   An autotrain stands at the down platform as a lady begins the ascent of the ramp. Such trains commonly turned back at South Harrow, but the complex crossover would allow them to do so here. (Lens of Sutton coll.)

56.   The north elevation is included to show the supplementary ticket windows and the massive sign facing users of Wembley Park. This footbridge does not appear in picture no. 52. Long disused, plans were made in 2004 for its demolition and replacement. An additional footbridge was also proposed in connection with the demands of the new stadium, then under construction, and a large shopping and residential development. (Lens of Sutton coll.)

57.   Rationalisation took place and all points were removed to reduce maintenance expenditure. The western footbridge was removed for the same reason. A DMU from Banbury is about to call on 26th April 1984, by which time the building had lost its neighbouring structures. (M.Turvey)

58. Bound for Aylesbury on 15th January 1992, no. 165003 is about to pass the reversing siding which had been laid on the site of the down main line. Work began behind the camera in the Autumn of 2004 to create a depot for storage and light maintenance of DMUs. Opening in June 2005, it was intended that it should reduce the increasing load on Aylesbury Depot and vacate the siding space at Marylebone in favour of additional platforms. (M.Turvey)

WEST OF WEMBLEY

59. Quadruple track extended from Neasden South Junction to Blind Lane box, a distance of two miles. The box had 20 levers and closed on 17th August 1977. (M.A.King/E.Hancock)

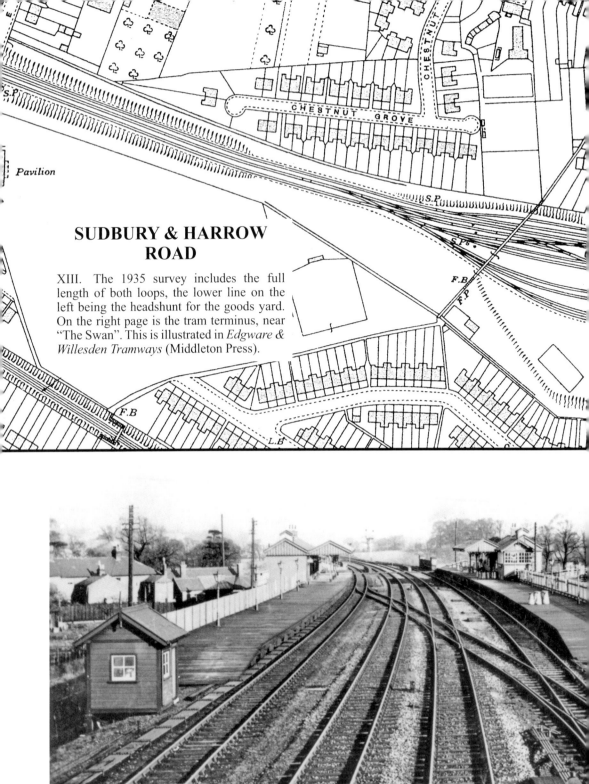

Pavilion

SUDBURY & HARROW ROAD

XIII. The 1935 survey includes the full length of both loops, the lower line on the left being the headshunt for the goods yard. On the right page is the tram terminus, near "The Swan". This is illustrated in *Edgware & Willesden Tramways* (Middleton Press).

CHESTNUT GROVE

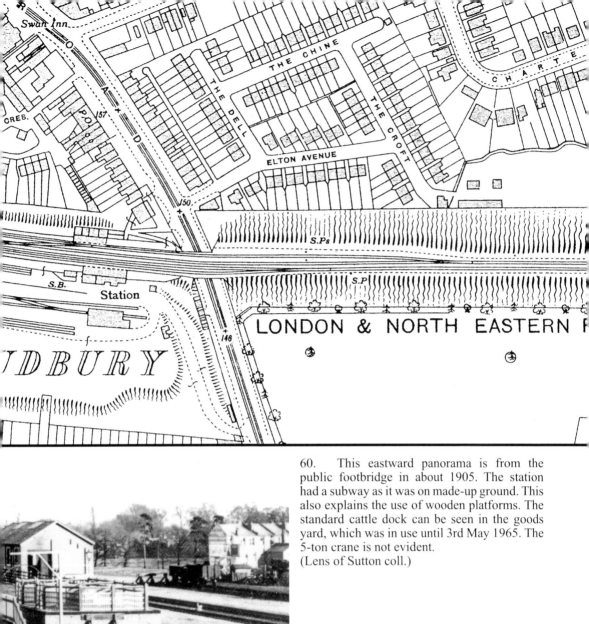

Swan Inn
CRES.
157
THE DELL
THE CHINE
THE CROFT
CHARTE
ELTON AVENUE
150
S.Ps
S.B.
Station
S.P.
DBURY
146
LONDON & NORTH EASTERN

60. This eastward panorama is from the public footbridge in about 1905. The station had a subway as it was on made-up ground. This also explains the use of wooden platforms. The standard cattle dock can be seen in the goods yard, which was in use until 3rd May 1965. The 5-ton crane is not evident.
(Lens of Sutton coll.)

61.   Running west sometime in the 1930s is class A5 4-6-2T no. 5451, one of a batch built for the GCR in 1911-23. On the right is the signal box, which had 46 levers and functioned until 2nd February 1969. (Lens of Sutton coll.)

62.   A Cup Final special heads east on 25th May 1963 behind ex-LMS class 5 no. 45335. The buildings and centre tracks were removed subsequently and the service reduced to peak hours only from 7th September 1964. The original platforms were later abandoned in favour of an island one linked to the subway. (L.W.Rowe/D.T.Rowe)

THE MASTER CUTLER
Restaurant Car Express
SHEFFIELD, NOTTINGHAM, LEICESTER, RUGBY, LONDON (Marylebone)

WEEKDAYS

	a.m.		p.m.
Sheffield (Victoria) ... dep	7 40	London (Marylebone) dep	6 15
Nottingham (Victoria) „	8 43	Rugby (Central) ... ... arr	8 6
Leicester (Central) ... „	9A18	Leicester (Central) ... „	8 31
Rugby (Central) ... ... „	9A46	Nottingham (Victoria) „	9 4
London (Marylebone)... arr	11A25	Sheffield (Victoria) ... „	10 11

A—On Saturdays departs Leicester (Central) 9 22, Rugby (Central) 9 52, and arrives London (Marylebone) 11 35 a.m.

THE SOUTH YORKSHIREMAN

BRADFORD, HUDDERSFIELD, SHEFFIELD, NOTTINGHAM, LEICESTER, LONDON (Marylebone)

WEEKDAYS

	a.m.		p.m.
Bradford (Exchange) ...dep	10 0	London (Marylebone) dep	4 50
Huddersfield ... ... „	10 35	Aylesbury ... ... „	5 49
Sheffield (Victoria) ... „	11 27		
	p.m.	Leicester (Central) ...arr	7 0
Nottingham (Victoria) „	12 30	Nottingham (Victoria) „	7 33
Loughborough (Central) „	12 52	Sheffield (Victoria) ... „	8 35
Leicester (Central) ... „	1 11	Penistone ... ... „	9 3
Rugby (Central) ... ... „	1 39	Huddersfield ... ... „	9 28
Aylesbury ... ... arr	2 29	Bradford (Exchange) ... „	10 10
London (Marylebone)... „	3 29		

Restaurant Cars available between Sheffield (Victoria) and London (Marylebone).

Passengers travelling from Bradford (Exchange), Huddersfield, Sheffield (Victoria) and London (Marylebone) by these services can reserve seats in advance on payment of a fee of 1s. 0d. per seat.

Summer 1951

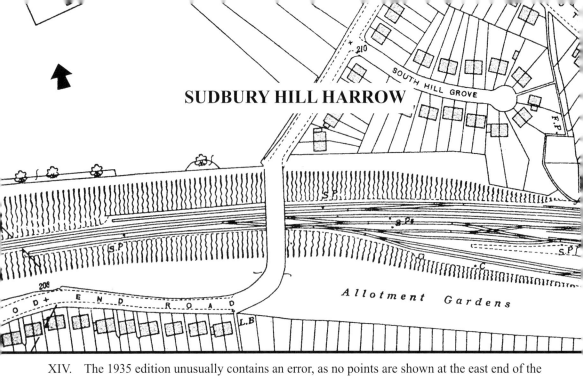

SUDBURY HILL HARROW

XIV.   The 1935 edition unusually contains an error, as no points are shown at the east end of the loops. The station was named "South Harrow" until 19th July 1926.

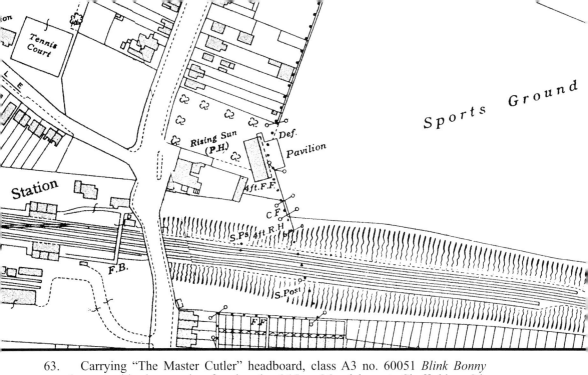

63.   Carrying "The Master Cutler" headboard, class A3 no. 60051 *Blink Bonny* speeds west with nine coaches forming the 6.15pm Marylebone to Sheffield on 8th June 1953. The signal box had a 54-lever frame. (N.W.Sprinks)

64.   Seen from the up platform are the points at the east end of the loops, together with the up crossover. Unusually slender posts supported Sugg's Rochester pattern gas lamps. When off peak services ceased to call from 7th September 1964, there continued to be an unadvertised service for school children on Tuesdays, Wednesdays and Thursdays only. (Lens of Sutton coll.)

65.   Class 4P 2-6-4T no. 42291 runs through with a train from Marylebone in June 1961. The booking office is visible below the arm on the lattice post. There are cattle pens in the goods yard, which received traffic until 3rd May 1965. A 5-ton crane was listed in 1938. (T.Wright)

66.   The booking office was at the end of the footbridge and at road level. The corbels and rainwater pipe indicate that there was once a substantial canopy on the gable end. The building was in commercial use in 2004. (E.Hancock coll.)

67.   Major changes took place and new platforms were built on the sites of the loops. The ramps were replaced by steps, as seen on 18th January 1994. A two-car Networker Turbo approaches, one of 28 such units in a 1992 contract. There were also 11 three-car sets. Five four-car class 168s were ordered in 1996. (F.Hornby)

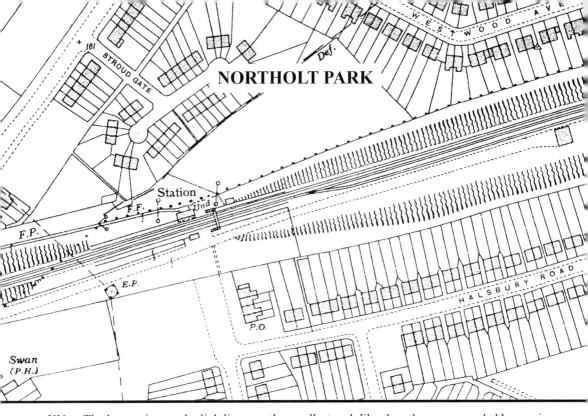

NORTHOLT PARK

XV.   The last station on the link line was the smallest and, like the others, surrounded by semi-detached houses. It opened on 19th July 1926 as "South Harrow & Roxteth" and was renamed on 13th May 1929.

68.   This 1969 photograph has the up platform on the left. Access to that side was by footpath only. The wooden building was replaced by a simple waiting shed by 1985.
(B.W.Leslie/GCR Society)

69.　　An up train runs in on 11th September 1997, by which time the service here was usually hourly and basic bus shelters were provided each side. (F.Hornby)

NORTHOLT JUNCTION

70.　　Our journey ends at the junction with the quadruple track of the main line at South Ruislip, as featured in our *Paddington to Princes Risborough* album. The route was exclusively GWR property southwards and joint with the GCR northwards. The down line from Neasden passes under the main lines and rises behind the signal box to the points on the right of this picture. A waste terminal (left) has occupied the site between the lines since 1980. Its connection is obscured by the signal post. The 29-lever signal box closed on 29th May 1990. South Ruislip had a basic service of two Marylebone trains per hour in 2004. (T.Wright)

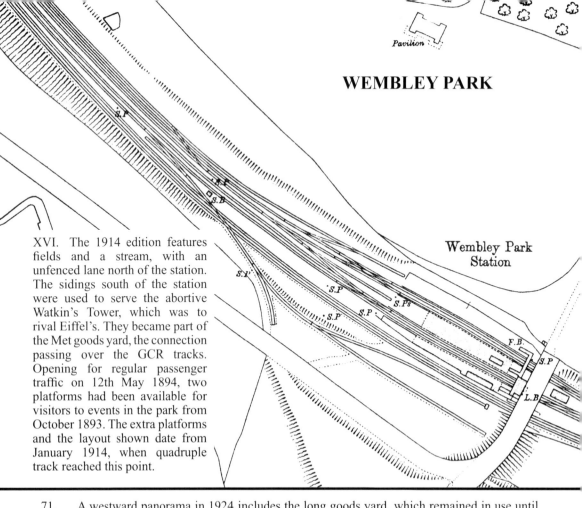

WEMBLEY PARK

Pavilion

Wembley Park
Station

XVI. The 1914 edition features fields and a stream, with an unfenced lane north of the station. The sidings south of the station were used to serve the abortive Watkin's Tower, which was to rival Eiffel's. They became part of the Met goods yard, the connection passing over the GCR tracks. Opening for regular passenger traffic on 12th May 1894, two platforms had been available for visitors to events in the park from October 1893. The extra platforms and the layout shown date from January 1914, when quadruple track reached this point.

71. A westward panorama in 1924 includes the long goods yard, which remained in use until 5th July 1965. Opened by the Met, traffic was transferred to the LNER on 1st December 1937. Quadrupling to Harrow-on-the-Hill of the electrified lines was completed on 10th January 1932. (A.A.Jackson/J.C.Gillham)

72.   Met no. 230 of 1929 T stock runs in from Watford on 6th April 1962. The signal box had a 59-lever frame, which was replaced by 47 push buttons on a desk on 28th September 1954. (J.C.Gillham)

73.   This spacious building was erected in 1923 in readiness for the British Empire Exhibition. The 1948 Olympic Games necessitated provision of a secondary booking office, an additional footbridge, a subway and new platform buildings plus canopies. The picture is from 1984. (D.Thompson)

74.   This westward panorama in October 2004 includes the carriage shed and was taken at the mid-point of a 12-month long major reconstruction. Pairs of platforms were closed for several months at a time, trains having to run non-stop. Maximum capacity would be increased from 22,000 passengers per hour to 37,500 in readiness for the completion of the new Wembley Stadium. (V.Mitchell)

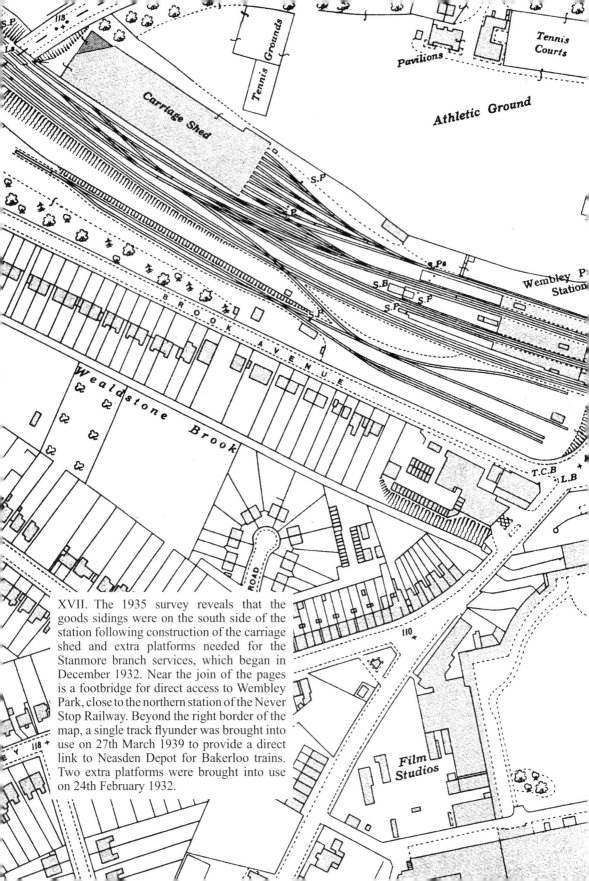

S.P

118

Tennis Grounds

Pavilions

Tennis Courts

Athletic Ground

Carriage Shed

S.P

S.P

Wembley P. Station

S.B

S.P

S.P

BROOK AVENUE

Wealdstone Brook

T.C.B

L.B

ROAD

110

XVII. The 1935 survey reveals that the goods sidings were on the south side of the station following construction of the carriage shed and extra platforms needed for the Stanmore branch services, which began in December 1932. Near the join of the pages is a footbridge for direct access to Wembley Park, close to the northern station of the Never Stop Railway. Beyond the right border of the map, a single track flyunder was brought into use on 27th March 1939 to provide a direct link to Neasden Depot for Bakerloo trains. Two extra platforms were brought into use on 24th February 1932.

118

Film Studios

T.C.B

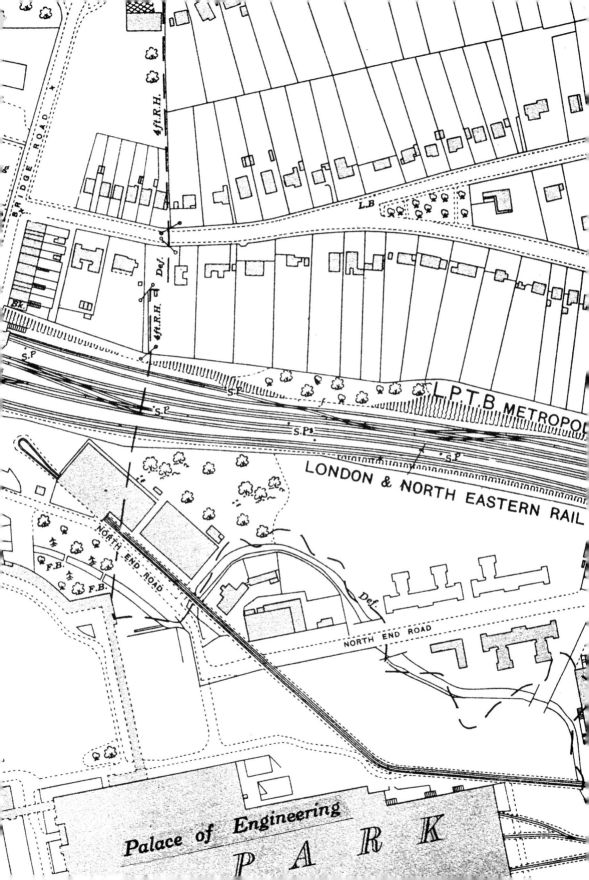

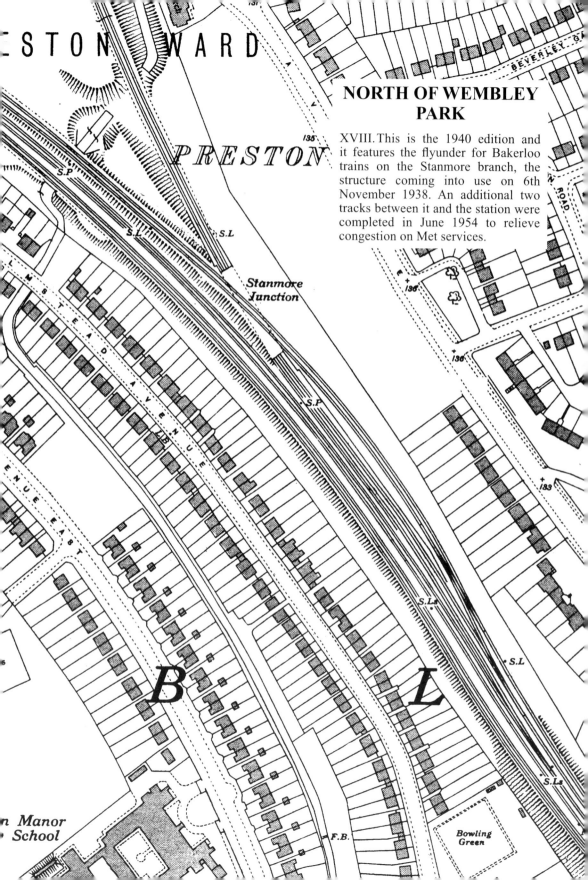

NORTH OF WEMBLEY PARK

XVIII. This is the 1940 edition and it features the flyunder for Bakerloo trains on the Stanmore branch, the structure coming into use on 6th November 1938. An additional two tracks between it and the station were completed in June 1954 to relieve congestion on Met services.

PRESTON ROAD

75.   Opened as a halt on 21st May 1908, an island platform was brought into use on 22nd November 1931, northbound, and 3rd January 1932, southbound. The first platforms had been built of timber to serve Uxendon Shooting Club. A train for Watford stops by the floral displays on 11th July 1997. (F.Hornby)

NORTHWICK PARK

76.   A halt named "Northwick Park & Kenton" came into use on 28th June 1923 and the platform was rebuilt as seen in around 1931 in readiness for quadruple electric tracks. The suffix was dropped in 1933. Access is from a subway that passes under all six lines. Departing on 2nd October 2004 is A stock *from* Aldgate. The non-electrified tracks are on the far left. Until the alterations to the electrified tracks at Harrow were completed after World War II, the up fast line crossed both slow ones on the level south of this station. (V.Mitchell)

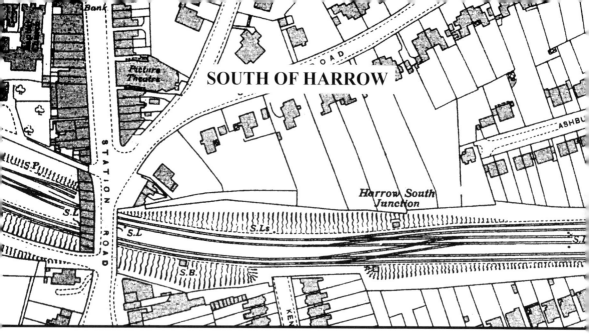

SOUTH OF HARROW

Harrow South
Junction

XIX.   Harrow South Junction was actually east of the station and is seen on the 1935 map at the point where six tracks converged to four. Rebuilding in 1938-39 resulted in six platforms, but six tracks through the station were not available until 1948.

77.   The short sidings on the left of the map were used for berthing locomotives between trips north (steam) and south (electric). All Aylesbury trains changed engines here from 1908 to 1925. On the left is Met 4-4-4T no. 105 taking coal. Also waiting is one of the batch of ten "Steeple Cab" or "Camelback" electric locomotives produced for the Met by Metro-Cammel in 1904. Loco change was at Wembley Park in 1904-08. (H.J.Patterson Rutherford/J.C.Gillham coll.)

HARROW-ON-THE-HILL

78.   The station was a terminus from 1880 to 1885 and became a junction for the Uxbridge branch on 4th July 1904. The suffix was added on 1st June 1894 and a subway was provided in 1908. (Lens of Sutton coll.)

79.   This is the London end of the station which was given two extra platforms on 21st June 1908, plus a 3-car bay for off-peak Uxbridge trains. The Harrow-Uxbridge section was electrified on 1st January 1905 and the route to Rickmansworth and Watford followed on 1st January 1925. (Lens of Sutton coll.)

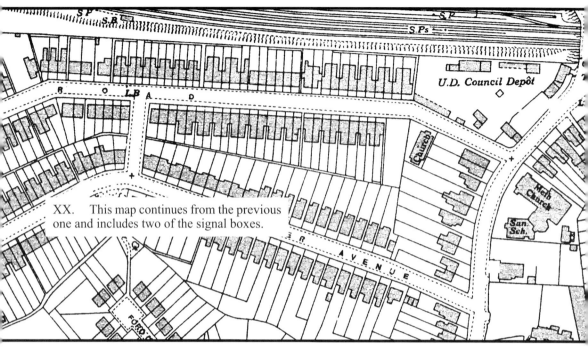

XX.   This map continues from the previous one and includes two of the signal boxes.

80.   The station was extensively rebuilt in 1938-39, although some of the work was not finished until long after the war. The south entrance is seen in 1987, not long before the bridge, together with the ticket office, was attached to a massive building development which included offices and retail units, formerly known as shops. The main entrance was by then on the north side. (D.Thompson)

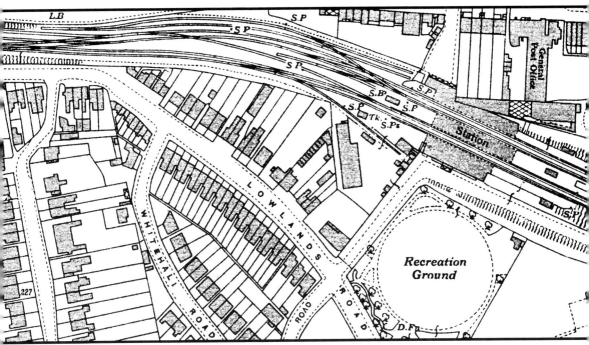

81. The scaffolding was in place on 29th May 1991 as a class 117 DMU was about to begin its non-stop run to Marylebone. The 1930s buildings were retained on all three island platforms. Some trains were hauled by class 47 diesels in 1991, as the DMUs had become so frail. (M.Turvey)

NORTH OF HARROW

82.   This westward panorama features a train from Rickmansworth or beyond approaching the up platform on which the photographer is standing. The goods yard is beyond Pinner Road bridge in the background. (H.J.Patterson Rutherford/J.C.Gillham coll.)

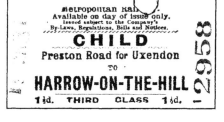

Metropolitan Rail.
Available on day of issue only.
Issued subject to the Company's
By-Laws, Regulations, Bills and Notices.
CHILD
Preston Road for Uxendon
TO
HARROW-ON-THE-HILL
1½d.   THIRD   CLASS   1½d.

2958

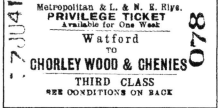

Metropolitan & L. & N. E. Rlys.
PRIVILEGE TICKET
Available for One Week
Watford
TO
CHORLEY WOOD & CHENIES
THIRD CLASS
SEE CONDITIONS ON BACK

078

7J04

83.   A view towards the station in 1924 includes much of the goods yard and indicates work in progress to prepare for a flyunder, which came into use on 14th September 1925. A further pair of tracks between the station and the junction came into use on 2nd May 1948. (Railway Engineer)

84.   Met F class 0-6-2T no. 91 is on the line from Uxbridge sometime in 1933 and Harrow North box is in the left background. The 6-ton crane can be seen in the goods yard, which was open until 3rd April 1967. (C.R.L.Coles)

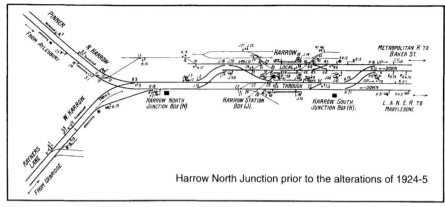

Harrow North Junction prior to the alterations of 1924-5

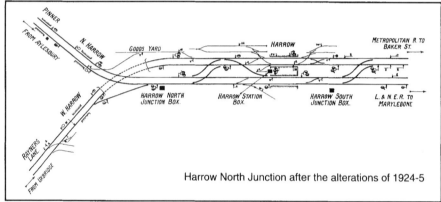

Harrow North Junction after the alterations of 1924-5

XXI. The diagrams show the position of the four platforms and three signal boxes, but do not have all the goods sidings. Quadrupling of the lines to Pinner and Watford South Junction took place in 1959-61. (London Railway Record)

85. A southward panorama from Pinner Road bridge on 26th November 1938 includes ex-Met locos, an 0-6-2T and a 4-4-4T. (Milepost 92½ coll.)

NORTH HARROW

86.   A halt was opened as a joint venture by the Met and GCR on 22nd March 1915. The early shelters were photographed in 1960, as a train departs for London. Little had changed more than 40 years later. (J.C.Gillham)

87.   New buildings were provided in 1931 at the time of road widening and provision of a new bridge. The main entrance is seen in February 1987. There had been a companion entrance to the south, until a second bridge was built in 1960-61. (D.Thompson)

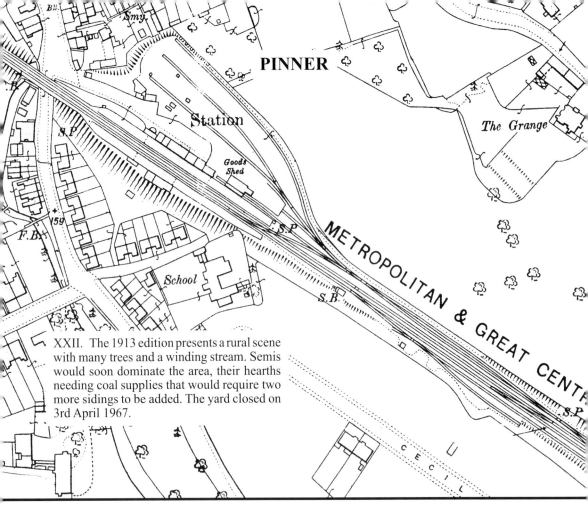

PINNER

Station

Goods Shed

The Grange

METROPOLITAN & GREAT CENTR

School

XXII. The 1913 edition presents a rural scene with many trees and a winding stream. Semis would soon dominate the area, their hearths needing coal supplies that would require two more sidings to be added. The yard closed on 3rd April 1967.

CECIL

88.   The station was a terminus from May 1885 until September 1887. Its main building was built on the north side and was photographed in 1987, having lost its chimney stacks. (D.Thompson)

89.   A view from an up train on 2nd September 1960 shows the ground being prepared behind the signal box for two new tracks for BR trains. A footpath from the down platform to Cecil Park had been created in about 1912 and so a subway had to be made for this. The signal box was closed on 28th January 1962, but had only been used to give goods trains access to the yard. (J.C.Gillham)

90.   The up side (left) retained much of its original character when photographed in 2004, along with the new footbridge which replaced a subway, the position of which is indicated by gaps in the conductor rails. The canopy on the right dates from 1961. (V.Mitchell)

NORTHWOOD HILLS

91.   We begin with two pictures from 25th August 1959. The station opened on 13th November 1933 to serve expanding suburbia. The admirable symmetry has been spoilt by official vandals in recent times. (J.C.Gillham)

92.   The additional two tracks would soon be laid on the ground in the foreground and the two-rail fence would be replaced by a brick wall, which begins at the left of the next picture. Note that the waiting room has solid fuel heating. (J.C.Gillham)

93.   A picture from 6th April 1962 shows A stock crossing from the new down line to the old one. The extra tracks between here and Northwood came into use on 5th February 1961. The crossover was temporary. The section to Harrow was available from 10th September 1961. (J.C.Gillham)

NORTHWOOD

XXIII. The 1913 survey shows the goods yard before its headshunt was extended under the bridge, lower right. Little else changed until the quadrupling of 1960.

94.	This photograph from the 1920s makes an interesting comparison with no. 88, as both buildings were erected in 1887 to the same basic plan. However, this was replaced by one on the bridge in the background on 15th January 1961. (Lens of Sutton coll.)

95.	The main difference from Pinner was the provision of a footbridge. Users of the down platform did not necessarily have to use it, as the footpath on the right gave direct access to Green Lane. (Lens of Sutton coll.)

96.   A southward panorama from the footbridge in August 1959 includes two electrified sidings for use by terminating trains. The running lines would soon only be used by through trains and the platforms would be removed. New platforms and the slow lines were laid on the site of the goods shed. The remaining part of the goods yard was in use until 14th November 1966. (J.C.Gillham)

97.   Looking south in October 2004 from the new down platform, we see a Turbo class 165 bound for Marylebone. A crossover and one siding was provided for terminating services. There was another siding from the latter serving a road/rail vehicle compound. (V.Mitchell)

MOOR PARK

98.   Opened as "Sandy Lodge" on 9th May 1910 to serve a golf course, the name was changed to "Moor Park & Sandy Lodge" on 18th October 1923. The suffix was dropped on 25th September 1950. The loco is ex-GCR class C4 4-4-2 no.2914. (H.C.Casserley)

99.   Timber platforms and shelters were still to be seen on 27th October 1956, as T stock of 1927 design ran in both directions. The station is still on the edge of woodland. There had been a goods siding until June 1938. (F.Hornby)

100.   The second island platform is seen under construction on 3rd September 1961; the first came into use on 23rd April 1961, together with the extra tracks southwards. The old up platform is in the background. Ground work for the quadrupling had begun in 1946. (J.C.Gillham)

XXIV. Simplified diagrams show the general scheme of the 1961 improvements. The Watford branch junctions were remotely controlled from Rickmansworth from the outset.
(Railway Magazine)

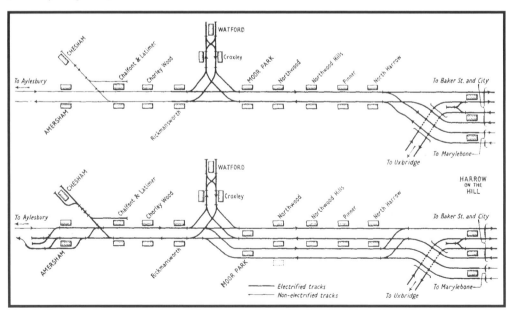

101.   The completed station had flat roof canopies over small waiting rooms, the ticket office being at the south end of the subway, which replaced the footbridge. About to run fast to Harrow-on-the-Hill on 22nd May 1999 is a train of A stock, capacious but with inexcusably noisy air compressors. (M.Turvey)

NORTH OF MOOR PARK

102.   The route passed over the River Colne after about half a mile, followed by the single line between Watford Junction and Rickmansworth Church Street. This is an eastward view in April 1962 and includes the replacement bridge spans for the slow lines, which were out of use from 1950 until June 1962. The branch is illustrated in our *Harrow to Watford* album. (J.C.Gillham)

103. The southern end of the triangular junction was also recorded in April 1962. The Rickmansworth lines pass under the bridge and the new up connection to the slow line is near the large sub-station building. The 20-lever Watford Road signal box had been in this vicinity. (J.C.Gillham)

104. South of the sub-station was the LT spoil tip, a facing siding diverging under the rear of the train in the previous picture. Ex-GWR 0-6-0PT no. 5786 numbered L92 by LT was recorded on 19th August 1969. The tip closed in 1970 and woodland grew over it. (H.McIntyre)

105. At the east end of the triangle, the lines of the Watford branch converge. The power cable bridge is seen from a train from Watford in April 1962. North curve carried a shuttle service in the early years and some Sunday trains in the 1940-50s ran between Watford and London via Rickmansworth. (J.C.Gillham)

CROXLEY

106.   We start with two photographs from March 1968 which show the 1925 structures in good condition, a comment that still applies. "Croxley Green" was used until 23rd May 1949, but there was another station of that name at the end of a BR branch from Watford Junction. There are still plans to link the two branches, despite a height difference of about 25ft. The other is illustrated in *Harrow to Watford*. (T.J.Edgington)

107.   The redundant signal box is seen at the north end of the down platform. It once controlled access to the goods yard, which closed on 14th November 1966. Its site is now occupied by a builders merchant. (T.J.Edgington)

XXV. The 1938 edition at 6ins to 1 mile did not include the sidings in the goods yard, but did show one to the canal and one passing through woodland before reversing into a gravel pit. These later branched off the east curve instead of the main line.

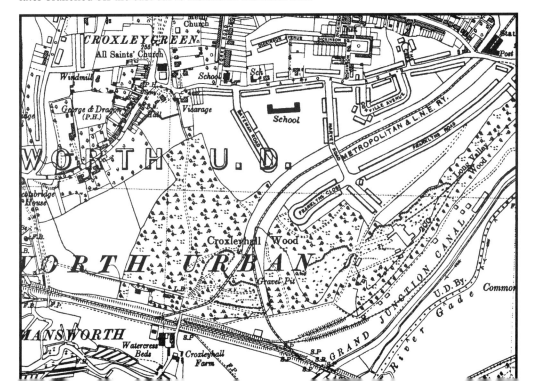

108.   The headboard STEAM ON THE MET 1989-1999 records an annual event which brought pleasure to so many. The train shuttled between Amersham and Watford on 22nd May 1999 and has GWR 0-6-0PT no. 9644 leading, followed by class 5 4-6-0 no. 45110 and ex-Met no. 12 *Sarah Siddons*. (M.Turvey)

NORTH OF CROXLEY

109.   Massive engineering was required to take the new branch across the Gade Valley. The contractors temporary bridge and railway was photographed in 1924.
(H.M.Pearson/R.S.Carpenter coll.)

110.   The bridge was recorded on 1st July 1989, together with ex-GWR no. 9466 passing over the Grand Union Canal. The River Gade passes under an arch to the right. The train includes NSE 4VEP unit no. 3457. (D.T.Rowe)

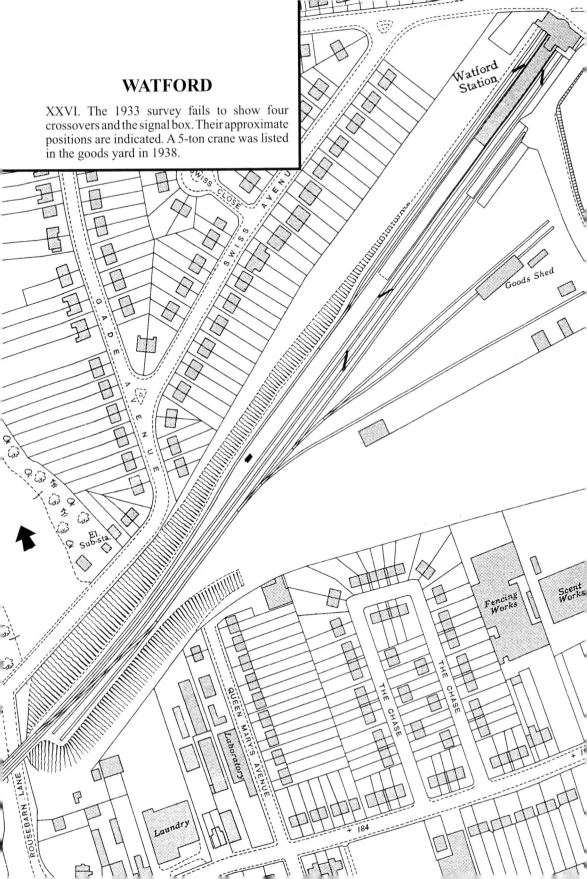

WATFORD

XXVI. The 1933 survey fails to show four crossovers and the signal box. Their approximate positions are indicated. A 5-ton crane was listed in the goods yard in 1938.

111.　The south elevation is nearing completion in 1924 in a residential area. The High Street had been the intended destination. The blocks in the foreground would support the platform and the large aperture was for the staircase to them. (H.M.Pearson/R.S.Carpenter coll.)

112.　The only item that is out of symmetry in this 1952 view is the cattle pen. The T stock motor coaches date from the 1927-32 period. (J.C.Gillham)

113.   Ten years later and little has changed, except that one crossover is visible. There are no details of the goods train or the surplus Bedford lorries. For many years, a goods train was scheduled to be here from 11.24am to 12.5pm. (J.C.Gillham)

114.   The north elevation again presented perfect symmetry. The design was simplified for Croxley and elaborated for Stanmore. The station was used by LNER trains in its first few months only. (F.Hornby)

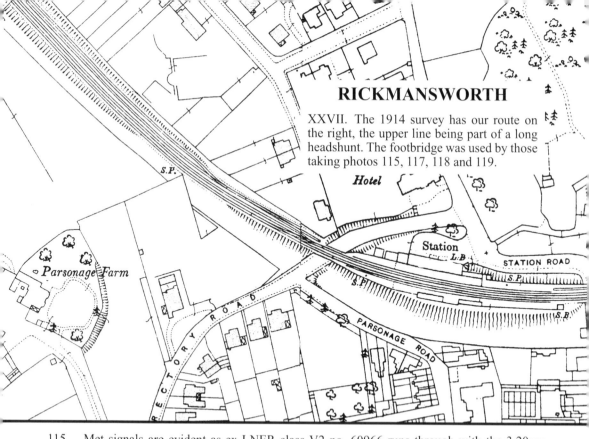

RICKMANSWORTH

XXVII. The 1914 survey has our route on the right, the upper line being part of a long headshunt. The footbridge was used by those taking photos 115, 117, 118 and 119.

115. Met signals are evident as ex-LNER class V2 no. 60966 runs through with the 3.20pm Marylebone to Manchester express on 9th September 1951, arrival being due at 9.51. The footboards in the up track were of benefit during loco changing operations. (N.W.Sprinks)

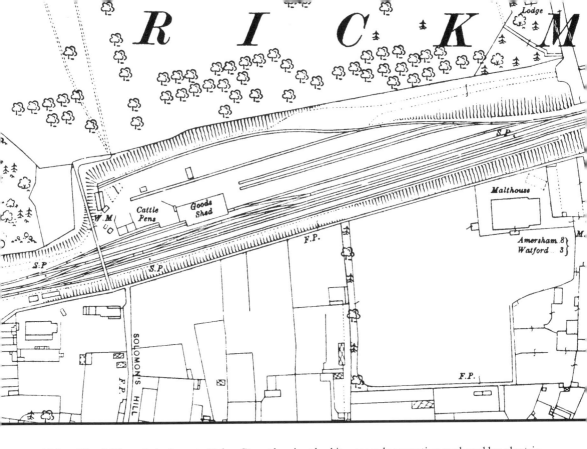

116.   The 9.30am Aylesbury to Baker Street has just had its steam locomotive replaced by electric no. 16 on 1st July 1951. It is in grey livery and devoid of a nameplate. (N.W.Sprinks)

117. From 1925 to 1962, all Aylesbury trains had their locomotives changed here. Waiting to run back onto a London train on 9th May 1959 are ex-Met locos no. 4 *Lord Byron* and no. 18 *Michael Faraday*. Visible in the mist are the crossovers, one devoid of conductor rails. (D.T.Rowe)

118. An example of the new A stock arrives from Baker Street shortly after electrification northwards in September 1961. In the distance are five berthing sidings; there are two more at the other end of the station, these being shown on the map. The goods yard closed on 14th November 1966. (P.J.Kelley)

119.   Midland trains were diesel hauled only occasionally, this example being no. D5000 with the 14.38 from Marylebone to Nottingham Victoria on 3rd September 1966 and this was its last day of operation. There were only three other through trains by that time. Coal is stacked high as yard closure is imminent. (T.Wright)

120.   The bay platform is seen more fully in picture 116. No. 165021 is bound for Marylebone on 23rd May 1992 and is passing an Amersham service. Two trains of each type per hour was the norm by that time. The signal box in the background took control of the area, including the Watford branch on 25th July 1955. The 1887 building survived, complete with chimneys, but the canopies were replaced in 1985, due to subsidence. We end our journey here over a healthy and well-kept railway. (M.Turvey)

MP Middleton Press

**Easebourne Lane, Midhurst
West Sussex. GU29 9AZ**

A-0 906520 B-1 873793 C-1 901706 D-1 904474

OOP Out of Print at time of printing - Please check current availability **BROCHURE AVAILABLE SHOWING NEW TITLES**
Tel:01730 813169   www.middletonpress.co.uk   email:info@middletonpress.co.uk